Cougars

Tracy C. Read

FIREFLY BOOKS

A FIREFLY BOOK

Published by Firefly Books Ltd. 2011

First Printing

Publisher Cataloging-in-Publication Data
(U.S.)
Read, Tracy C.
    Exploring the world of cougars /
  Tracy C. Read.
[ ] p. : col. photos. ;   cm.
Includes index.
Summary: The cougar is revealed in color photography and insightful information.
ISBN-13: 978-1-55407-785-4 (bound)
ISBN-10: 1-55407-785-0 (bound)
ISBN-13: 978-1-55407-956-8 (pbk.)
ISBN-10: 1-55407-956-X (pbk.)
1. Puma. I. Title.
599.7424 dc22   QL737.C23R434 2011

Library and Archives Canada Cataloguing in
Publication
Read, Tracy C.
    Exploring the world of cougars /
  Tracy C. Read.
Includes index.
ISBN-13: 978-1-55407-785-4 (bound)
ISBN-10: 1-55407-785-0 (bound)
ISBN-13: 978-1-55407-956-8 (pbk.)
ISBN-10: 1-55407-956-X (pbk.)
1. Puma--Juvenile literature. I. Title.
QL737.C23R43 2011   j599.75'24
C2011-9023385

Published in the United States by
Firefly Books (U.S.) Inc.
P.O. Box 1338, Ellicott Station
Buffalo, New York 14205

Published in Canada by
Firefly Books Ltd.
66 Leek Crescent
Richmond Hill, Ontario L4B 1H1

The Publisher gratefully acknowledges the financial support for our publishing program by the Government of Canada through the Canada Book Fund as administered by the Department of Canadian Heritage.

Cover and interior design by
Janice McLean/Bookmakers Press Inc.

Printed in Canada

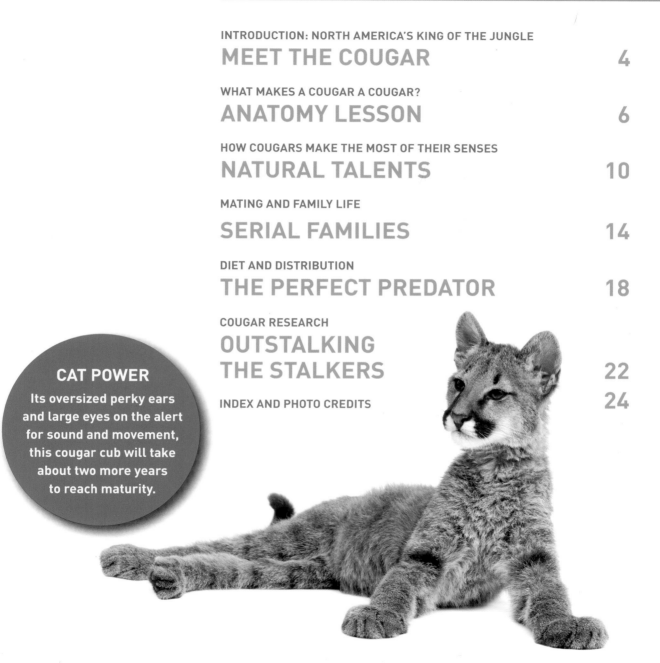

CONTENTS

CAT POWER

Its oversized perky ears and large eyes on the alert for sound and movement, this cougar cub will take about two more years to reach maturity.

MEET THE COUGAR

Strong, silent and savvy, the cougar prowls its territory with the grace of a domestic cat and the confidence of an African lion. It quietly combs trails, forests, clearings and underbrush in its search for prey. After an explosive takedown of a large hoofed mammal, such as a deer or moose, *Puma concolor* ("cat of one color") feasts on meat. Then this secretive cat vanishes as if into thin air. Only the remains of the kill and perhaps a paw print or two linger as proof that this long, lean hunter was ever there.

The cougar is one of three members of the wild-cat family (Felidae) still commonly found in the United States and Canada. The other two are the lynx (*Lynx canadensis*), which lives in Alaska and northern Canada, and the bobcat (*Lynx rufus*), found in the lower 48 states and southern Canada.

But, without question, the king of these cats is the cougar, the largest free-ranging cat in North America. Native Americans revered the cougar as the "lord of the forest" and the "cat of god." Bigger and faster than its two smaller cousins, the cougar can outrun, outjump and outkill them. And even though humans continue to whittle away at its habitat, the cougar has the greatest distribution of any land mammal in the New World.

Let's find out how the cat of one color has managed to succeed in its changing landscape.

THE GHOST CAT

The wary cougar avoids human contact when it can. In fact, many researchers and biologists who have spent their lives studying this wild cat (also known as mountain lion and puma, among a host of other common names) have rarely observed one in its natural habitat.

ANATOMY LESSON

LICKED CLEAN

Cougars range in color from brown, tan or tawny to silver-gray. After feeding, below, this cat cleans off all remnants of its prey using its rough tongue. It also spends hours keeping its fur free of dirt and mud.

By night, the cougar inhabits a shadowy world, its eyes wide open and its ears alert, its long, thick tail a fluid extension of its lean, well-built body. Its large, padded paws are equipped with lethal claws that are sheathed and protected until needed; its athletic hindquarters are always primed for action. This big, self-sufficient cat is designed to hunt alone.

A number of physical adaptations contribute to the puma's impressive success as a hunter, allowing it to do battle with much larger animals. Because its rear legs are longer than its forelimbs, it can navigate rugged, uneven terrain with ease, and it walks on its tiptoes to fully exploit the length of its legs.

Like those of other cats, the cougar's front limbs are attached to well-muscled shoulder blades. This, in combination with a strong, flexible spine, enables it to lengthen its stride and quickly change direction as it chases its prey.

With a relatively small lung capacity for its size, the cougar employs quick decisive bursts of speed when giving chase. It grasps its prey with its muscular forearms, sharp claws exposed. Then, opening its short jaws, it delivers deep, stabbing bites to the neck, head or throat with its robust canine teeth. A quick kill ends any risk of injury to the cougar.

THE GREAT LEAP FORWARD

Like all cats, the tree-climbing cougar does some rapid strategic calculations before making its move. Then it deploys its powerful haunches, propelling itself through the air toward its target. A cougar is capable of vertical jumps as high as 15 feet (4.5 m).

The cougar's short, muscular front legs, flexible wrists and huge feet are designed for holding prey and climbing trees and cliffsides.

HOW A COUGAR CHANGES ITS SPOTS

A cougar kitten is born fur-covered, its coat dotted with black spots until the third or fourth month. Black rings encircle its tail, and it has dark facial markings.

Fur
The cougar's dense fur varies in length, depending on habitat and season, keeping it warm in cold climates.

Weight
A male cougar weighs between 110 and 232 pounds (50-105 kg); the female is 79 to 132 pounds (36-60 kg).

Let your backbone slide
A supple spine allows the cougar to stretch, arch and twist as it subdues prey or struggles with predators.

Speed demon
A cougar has been clocked doing the 100-yard dash in under 5 seconds, tearing up the turf at 45 miles per hour (72 km/h).

Tenacious tail
The cougar uses its thick, muscular tail for balance, especially when leaping. The tail accounts for about one-third of the cougar's total length.

Length from nose tip to tip of tail
Male: 6 to 9.5 feet (1.8-2.9 m).
Female: 5.2 to 7.2 feet (1.6-2.2 m).

Height
A male cougar measures from 22 to 31 inches (56-79 cm) at the shoulder; the female is 21 to 30 inches (53-76 cm).

Ears
The cougar's ears are short and rounded. Later in life, the male's ears are notched and battle-scarred from fighting.

Eyes
Blue at birth, the cougar's eyes turn grayish brown to golden at about five months. Its pupils are oval-shaped.

Teeth
Packed into the cougar's short jaws are 30 teeth, including four extra-long, extremely strong canines, which it can drive into the spine of its prey.

Paws
Big and meaty, a cougar's paws have sharp claws that are hidden when it walks or is resting but emerge when it is taking down prey or climbing a tree.

9

NATURAL TALENTS

A solitary hunter like the cougar calls on its physical strength and stamina to wrestle prey to the ground. But this predator possesses other vital traits that influence how *Puma concolor* survives in its world.

Active at night and during the twilight hours of dawn and dusk, the cougar relies on its keen vision to make its way along forest edges and over rocky ground as daylight fades. Its eyes, compared with those of other carnivores, are big for its size, and they have a number of adaptations that ensure high performance in low-light conditions.

Oval pupils open wide in the darkness to let in roughly three times as much light as do human eyes. (In the bright light of day, the pupils narrow to slits.) The retina, located at the back of the eye, is filled with nerve cells called rods, which function best in dim light, and as with many other night-hunting animals, the cougar's eye features a layer of tissue called the tapetum lucidum, which reflects light back into the eye.

Forward-looking eyes allow the cougar to focus on one thing with both eyes. Known as binocular vision, this attribute provides excellent depth perception, which is critical when the cougar is struggling with its prey. The cougar has good peripheral vision as well, which means it can also see what's happening to its left and right.

WALK SOFTLY
How does such a big cat track its prey without being detected? The master of stealthy stalking, the puma prowls on paws that feature outsized toe and heel pads and soft fur that deadens the sound of its footfall.

PUMA POUNCE

In fierce concentration, a cougar launches itself forward in a sudden burst of speed while pursuing its prey.

If you've ever watched a domestic cat's dramatic response to even the slightest sound, you'll agree that cats have highly sensitive hearing. Researchers have limited access to cougars in the wild, so based on information gathered about other members of the cat family, which hear higher sound frequencies than humans do, they have concluded that this big cat's sense of hearing is an important weapon in its hunting arsenal.

Because the puma is able to detect and locate prey that has tucked itself away for the night, researchers believe that the cougar's sense of smell plays a part in boosting its hunting handicap, although testing its sense of smell is a challenge.

A cougar, of course, craves the taste of meat. And, enhancing its perception at close range, long whiskers that grow on its muzzle send messages via touch and air flow. These help the cat quickly fine-tune its approach to prey. Aided by this information, the puma targets its killing bite.

HEARING
Its rounded, cupped ear flaps swivel in different directions to gather and direct sound to the inner ears.

SIGHT
The night-hunting cougar sees remarkably well in low lighting and has good peripheral vision.

SMELL
While its sense of smell is not strong, the cougar has no trouble finding sleeping prey at night.

TASTE
Like all carnivores, the cougar has a wide-ranging appetite for fresh meat.

TOUCH
A healthy growth of long muzzle whiskers helps the cougar navigate in the dark.

SERIAL FAMILIES

Adult cougars of both sexes spend most of their lives just trying to avoid one another — except when they are on the lookout for breeding partners.

Cougars are able to mate and reproduce all year round, but more than 70 percent of North American cougar births take place from May through October. This may be because other animals are having offspring then, creating a ready food supply for the young cougar family.

How do the male and female make contact? As a male cougar travels through his territory, he leaves scented scrapes — kicked-up piles of earth — along his route. These scrapes are messages to other cougars, perhaps warnings to rival males, and they also attract the attention of females whose home ranges occur within the male's territory.

A cougar vocalizes by purring, growling, hissing, snarling and

CAT CAVES

Cougars do not mate for life or even for a single season, and they may have multiple partners, but the female takes full responsibility for feeding and rearing her young. At right, a mother puma and a juvenile cozy up for a nap on a secure cliffside ledge.

PROTECTIVE CUSTODY
When home security is threatened by strangers, a mother cougar relocates her young cubs to a new nursery, one kitten at a time.

spitting, but when a female signals her breeding availability, the message is crystal-clear. She unleashes an unearthly scream known as a caterwaul. If more than one male responds, a vicious, dangerous competition may follow, and the defeated male limps away bearing the marks of a hard-fought battle — or worse.

After an intense mating period that can last for a day or as long as two weeks, both the male and the female move on, perhaps to be with other partners. The male has no relationship with his offspring; his central goal is to reproduce with as many females as possible.

As an insurance policy, the female puma often maintains a warm relationship with this male as well as other area males. Strange males have a tendency to kill and eat cougar cubs that are not their own, and they may also harm an unknown female that is protecting her cubs.

Setting up a nursery that is out of sight, preferably concealed by rocks or tree branches, the mother gives birth to two or three kittens roughly 92 days after mating. Newborns are blind, tiny and helpless. Their eyes open after two weeks, and by four weeks, the cubs are on their feet and eager to explore their surroundings. At this point, they are also ready to start learning the lessons that will help them survive as young cougars. Play fights with siblings promote physical and mental development.

In another month or so, the cubs are strong enough to follow their mother to feed at an animal she has killed. At five months, they can climb trees to evade predators and their hunting skills continue to develop. Between the ages of one and two years, they are almost fully grown and ready for independence. Female subadults may stay in the vicinity, but males typically establish territories farther off.

THE PERFECT PREDATOR

LONG IN THE TOOTH

The cougar's four prominent canine teeth are extremely strong and resistant to breaking. Traveling easily over rough terrain, this agile cat boosts its hunting success by blending into the background.

Just over a hundred years ago, the cougar could be found throughout most of the New World, from the Atlantic Ocean to the Pacific, from sea level to 14,765 feet (4,500 m) and from the Far North to the tip of South America. This skilled carnivore lived in forests, foothills, mountains, rainforests, plains and deserts — in every ecosystem but the Arctic tundra. Then, as now, the cougar specialized in hunting deer and elk, adding smaller mammals, such as snowshoe hares, rabbits, porcupines, beavers, raccoons and mice, to its all-meat diet when necessary.

But by the late 20th century, this mighty cat's range had been trimmed to one-third its former size. In North America, the human drive to tame and occupy the vast wilderness pushed the cougar farther and farther west. Today, in the east, only a tiny cougar population survives in Florida.

A big cat needs room to roam, as do the big animals it likes to eat. From northern British Columbia to Chile, the cougar continues to carve out a living in great spans of rugged mountains, forested foothills and desert scrublands, with male cougars fighting for territorial dominance of areas that range from roughly 60 to 270 square miles (155-700 sq km). One of those territories may encompass the smaller home ranges of several females.

A hunting cougar must always

CATCHING BIG AIR

Springing up and forward using
its powerful haunches, the cougar
relies on its long, thick tail for
balance. Its big, padded front paws
act as brakes when it lands.
The cougar's record for the
running long jump is a
remarkable 45 feet (13.7 m).

weigh the advantage of being able to see against the disadvantage of being seen. In desert and mountainous habitat, the cougar's tawny color helps it disappear into the neutral background. At forest edges and in scrubland, the cougar relies on the concealing cover of grasses, bushes and trees.

Along its hunting route, a cougar makes a series of brief stops to lie in wait for passing prey. It sits quietly, alert to movement and sounds around it. If it spots an opportunity, the puma employs its trademark stalk-and-ambush hunting style. The shorter the distance between puma and prey, the higher its rate of success, which makes

this cat's skill at a silent approach all the more important. After creeping as close as it can, the cougar furiously rushes its victim, sometimes leaping onto its back.

Since its favorite fare is large hoofed mammals that may well be sporting heavy antlers or horns, the cougar tries to customize its killing bite to suit the circumstance. A quick, suffocating attack on the

throat of a massive elk might save the cougar from having its head frantically bashed in by hooves or antlers. Smaller animals can be stopped with a spine-breaking bite to the back of the neck.

Even so, going up against big game is always dangerous, especially on steep terrain. Occasionally, both cougar and prey may tumble to their death.

VANISHING POINT

Such human activities as farming, forestry and mining have gobbled up cougar habitat. Occasionally, the typically shy cougar may be tempted to go pet hunting in a nearby suburban neighborhood. Attacks on people are rare, but they can be fatal.

WHAT'S ON THE MENU?

A cougar dines on whatever prey is available, though the more experienced hunter chooses to stalk large hoofed mammals, like deer, elk, moose and sheep. (Young and old animals are easier to take down.) Smaller animals, such as rabbits, raccoons, porcupines, birds and reptiles, fill in the gaps for both the seasoned hunter and the beginner.

CATCH AS CAT CAN

A mother cougar shares dinner with her juvenile offspring. After taking down its prey, a cougar may drag it up to 85 yards (78 m) away and stash it under protective vegetation. Eating its fill, the cougar then covers the leftovers with leaves or branches, returning for seconds when its stomach empties.

OUTSTALKING THE STALKERS

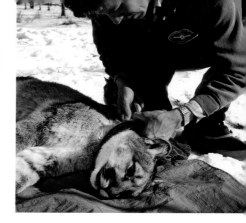

In the New World, stories passed down by Native Americans and European settlers about the great cat that stalked the wilderness served as a starting place in our understanding of *Puma concolor*. But this cat's sheer elusiveness has always presented scientists with a unique challenge: How do we study an animal that lives most of its life out of sight?

The inevitable competition for land and food between people and wild animals eventually resulted in campaigns to eliminate the cougar and other carnivores from the landscape. Even so, the bodies of *Puma concolor* killed by hired government agents served as an early source of hard facts about the cougar's physical characteris-

tics and diet. Field studies by wildlife biologists and amateur naturalists in the early decades of the 20th century contributed additional insights, but it was American Maurice Hornocker's groundbreaking work in Idaho in the 1960s and 1970s that set a new standard for cougar research.

Hornocker pioneered live-capture techniques: Cougars were tracked and treed by trained dogs and sedated with tranquilizing guns. Researchers could then safely record each cat's physical statistics and fit the cougar with a numbered collar that would identify it for future meetings, also enabled through the use of tracking hounds. In this way, Hornocker began to amass details

about the big cat's home ranges and the effect of its hunting behavior on prey species.

In 1973, John Seidensticker fine-tuned the approach by fitting sedated cougars with radio collars. These collars allowed researchers to pick up a cougar's exact location and to monitor its movements. Researchers in both

the United States and Canada eagerly took up these methods in the following decades.

Recent technologies are creating a more textured portrait of the cougar. Among these are camera traps that snap surveillance photos of the cougar as it travels, global positioning systems that can document an individual's daily habits, DNA analysis and more efficient methods of sharing and updating data.

Today, most of us recognize the value of managing wildlife populations. Thanks to the work of dedicated researchers, the majestic cat of one color may well roam the wilderness for centuries to come.

PHOTOS © SHUTTERSTOCK
p. 3 Eric Isselée
p. 6 top: anyaivanova
p. 6 bottom: pixelparticle
p. 7 creativex
p. 8 inset: Joel Bauchat Grant
p. 9 Eric Isselée
p.12 S.R. Maglione
p.13 Helen E. Grose
p.14 left: Eric Isselée
p.14 inset right: JKlingebiel
p.15 Chris Curtis
p.17 Geoffrey Kuchera
p.18 bottom: CatonPhoto
p.19 Dennis Donohue
p.20 top: Shawn Kashou
p.20 left: Geoffrey Kuchera
p.20 snowshoe hare: nialat
p.20 bighorn sheep: Rafa Irusta
p.21 raccoon: karamysh
p.21 sheep: hraska
p.21 porcupine:
    Caroline Vancoillie
p.21 moose: Tony Campbell
p.21 white-tail deer:
    Thomas Pettengill

PHOTOS © WAYNE LYNCH
p.18 top
p.22 both
p.23

PHOTOS © TIM FITZHARRIS
p. 5
p.11
p.16
p.21 top